BUG BOOKS

Woodlouse

Revised and Updated

Stephanie St. Pierre

Heinemann
LIBRARY

www.heinemann.co.uk/library

Visit our website to find out more information about Heinemann Library books.

To order:

☎ Phone 44 (0) 1865 888066

🖹 Send a fax to 44 (0) 1865 314091

🖥 Visit the Heinemann Bookshop at www.heinemann.co.uk/library to browse our catalogue and order online.

First published in Great Britain by Heinemann Library, Halley Court, Jordan Hill, Oxford OX2 8EJ, part of Harcourt Education.
Heinemann is a registered trademark of Harcourt Education Ltd.

Editorial: Diyan Leake and Catherine Clarke
Design: Kimberly R. Miracle and Cavedweller Studio
Illustration: David Westerfield
Picture research: Melissa Allison
Production: Alison Parsons

Originated by Dot Gradations Ltd
Printed and bound in China by South China Printing Company

ISBN 978 0 431 01983 3 (hardback)
12 11 10 09 08
10 9 8 7 6 5 4 3 2 1

ISBN 978 0 431 01989 5 (paperback)
12 11 10 09 08
10 9 8 7 6 5 4 3 2 1

British Library Cataloguing in Publication Data
St. Pierre, Stephanie.
Woodlouse. - 2nd Edition. - (Bug Books)
595.3'72
A full catalogue record for this book is available from the British Library.

Acknowledgements
The publishers would like to thank the following for permission to reproduce photographs:
© Animals Animals (Donald Specker) pp. **4**, **7**; © Bruce Coleman pp. **6** (Robert Dunne), **10** (Dwight Kuhn); © Corbis pp. **17**, **18**, **19**; © Dwight Kuhn pp. **8**, **15**, **21**, **26**, **27**, **29**; © James P. Rowan pp. **20**, **23**; © James Rowan pp. **14**, **22**; © NHPA pp. **11**, **12**; © Oxford Scientific Films (Robert Jackman) p. **28**; © Peter Arnold Inc. (Clyde H. Smith) p. **5**; © Photolibrary (Barrie Watts) p. **9**; © Photo Researchers Inc. pp. **13** (Biophoto Associates), **16** (G. Buttner/Naturbild/Okapia), **24** (Holt Studios International), **25** (Ken Brate).

Cover photograph of a pill woodlouse reproduced with permission of Photolibrary.com (Marshall Black).

The publishers would like to thank James Rowan and Lawrence Bee for their assistance in the preparation of the first edition of this book.

Every effort has been made to contact copyright holders of any material reproduced in this book. Any omissions will be rectified in subsequent printings if notice is given to the publishers.

Contents

Some words are shown in bold, **like this**. You can find out what they mean by looking in the glossary.

What are woodlice?

shell

leg

Woodlice are small grey bugs. They are not **insects**. They are **crustaceans**. They have seven pairs of legs and a rounded shell.

4

A woodlouse's shell is called an **exoskeleton**. The exoskeleton (shell) protects the soft parts of the woodlouse's body.

What do woodlice look like?

Woodlice have two short **antennae**. The woodlice in this book are a special type. They are called **pillbugs**.

Pillbugs roll up into little balls when they are in danger. They look like little pills. They are the size of a pea.

How are woodlice born?

Female woodlice lay eggs. Most woodlice have two **broods** of young each year. They have one brood in the spring and another in the summer.

egg

Woodlice eggs **hatch** in a **pouch** in their mother's belly. There can be 200 eggs in the pouch. They hatch after three to seven weeks.

baby woodlouse

egg

How do woodlice grow?

The **female** woodlouse carries her babies in a **pouch** for over a month. The babies are white and their bodies are soft. They only have six pairs of legs.

old skin

new skin

As the woodlice grow, their shells get too tight. The old shell falls off and there is a new one underneath. This is called **moulting**.

adult

baby

When woodlice **moult** for the first time they grow another pair of legs. Now they have seven pairs, like an adult. Woodlice moult a few times before they are fully grown.

Baby woodlice are very pale. Their shells get harder and darker each time they moult.

shell

How do woodlice move?

Woodlice crawl. They move very slowly. They cannot run away from danger. **Pillbugs** can roll up instead of running away.

pillbug

Woodlice are **nocturnal**. This means they usually only move around at night. During the day they often sleep under rocks and logs.

What do woodlice eat?

This pile of grass clippings makes a perfect meal for woodlice. Woodlice also eat dead leaves and old fruit. They even eat rotting logs.

Sometimes woodlice eat growing plants. Woodlice can damage plants if they eat their roots and new leaves.

roots

Which animals eat woodlice?

shrew

Woodlice have many enemies. **Shrews**, toads, frogs, and lizards eat woodlice. Small owls and some foxes also eat them.

Spiders, centipedes, and some beetles also eat woodlice. Woodlice even eat other woodlice that are **moulting**.

centipede

Where do woodlice live?

Most **crustaceans** live in water. Woodlice live on land but they need to stay **moist**. If they get too dry they will die.

Woodlice choose **damp** places to live. They live under rocks, in dead logs, and in other dark cool places. They usually die if they come indoors.

How long do woodlice live?

Woodlice can live for up to five years. Most of them do not live that long. They must watch out for enemies and be careful not to get too dry.

A **female** woodlouse has her first
babies when she is two years old.
In her lifetime, she can have more
than 1,000 babies!

What do woodlice do?

Woodlice **recycle**. Woodlice help to make the soil richer by eating dead plants. This helps new plants to grow.

24

Woodlice do not do much when it is cold. They hide under rocks and logs and stay still until the weather warms up.

Why are woodlice special?

Pillbugs roll up when they are disturbed. You can pick one up gently and see how it rolls.

You can keep woodlice as pets. Keep them in a jar with holes in the lid. Put some **damp** soil in the jar. Feed your woodlice leaves and potato peelings. Spray the jar with water every week.

Thinking about woodlice

Which of these animals is related to the woodlouse? Can you think of any other animals that have an **exoskeleton** (shell)?

This boy wants to keep some woodlice as pets. Where should he look for them? What should he feed them?

Bug map

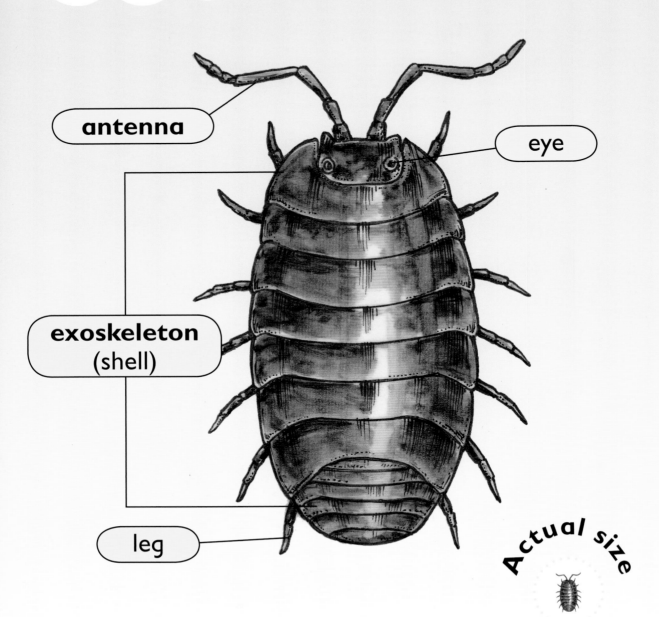

antenna

eye

exoskeleton
(shell)

leg

Actual size

30

Glossary

antenna (more than one = antennae) thin tube that sticks out from the head of an insect. Antennae can be used to smell, feel, hear, or sense direction.

brood group of babies that hatch at the same time

crustacean relative of insects that has a tough shell. Woodlice, shrimp, lobsters, and crabs are all crustaceans.

damp a little bit wet

exoskeleton hard shell on the outside of an animal's body

female animal that can lay eggs or give birth to young. Women are females.

hatch break out of an egg

insect small animal with six legs and a body with three parts

moist slightly wet

moulting time in an insect's life when it gets too big for its skin. The old skin drops off and a new one is underneath.

nocturnal being active at night, and sleeping during the day

pillbug type of woodlouse that rolls up into a little ball when it is disturbed

pouch baggy area of skin where a mother carries her young

recycle take waste and make it into something useful

shrew animal that is related to a mole. It eats insects and other bugs.

31

Index

More books to read

First Library of Knowledge: World of Bugs, Nicholas Harris
    (Blackbirch Press, 2006)
Minibeasts: Going on a Bug Hunt, Stewart Ross and Jim Pipe
    (Franklin Watts, 2006)
Woodlice Up Close, Greg Pyres (Raintree, 2005)